SCHOLASTIC
News
Nonfiction Readers

D0001125

Let's Be Friends

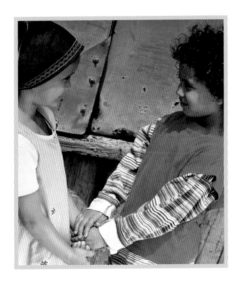

By Amanda Miller

Children's Press®
An Imprint of Scholastic Inc.
New York Toronto London Auckland Sydney
Mexico City New Delhi Hong Kong
Danbury, Connecticut

These content vocabulary word builders are for grades 1–2.

Subject Consultant: Eli J. Lesser, MA, Director of Education, National Constitution Center, Philadelphia, Pennsylvania

Reading Consultant: Cecilia Minden-Cupp, PhD, Early Literacy Consultant and Author, Chapel Hill, North Carolina

Art Direction and Production: Scholastic Classroom Magazines

Library of Congress Cataloging-in-Publication Data

Miller, Amanda, 1974-
Let's be friends / Amanda Miller.
    p. cm. – (Scholastic news nonfiction readers)
Includes bibliographical references and index.
ISBN 13: 978-0-531-21344-5 (lib. bdg.)   978-0-531-21444-2 (pbk.)
ISBN 10: 0-531-21344-7 (lib. bdg.)   0-531-21444-3 (pbk.)
1. Friendship in children–Juvenile literature. 2. Friendship–Juvenile literature.
I. Title. II. Series.
BF723.F68M55 2009   158.2'5–dc22 2009007317

3 4 5 6 7 8 9 10 R 18 17 16 15 14 13 12   62

CONTENTS

Who Are Your Friends?

Look around. Do you see your **friends**?

Friends are people you like to be with. Friends make you happy.

When was the last time you made a new friend?

friends

Your school **playground** is a good place for making friends. Ask someone new to play!

If a child asks you to play, say, "Yes." If you are already playing with friends, say, "Join us!"

You can all be friends.

You might make some new friends at the playground.

playground

What Friends Do

Friends make each other **laugh**. Anna tells Alex a funny joke. Then Alex does a funny dance.

That's what friends do!

laugh

What do you like to
do with your friends?

9

Friends help each other.

Amy helps Jake finish the **puzzle**. Jake helps Amy reach the book on the top shelf.

That's what friends do!

puzzle

A big puzzle goes faster with a friend.

Sometimes a friend may feel sad.

When Ben is sad, Lilly wants him to feel better. Lilly tries to make him **smile**!

That's what friends do.

smile

When you are sad, it helps to have a friend.

Staying Friends

When friends want the same thing, they **share**.

Sometimes Grace gets the bigger piece of the last cookie. Sometimes Jen gets the bigger piece.

That's how they stay friends.

share

Would you share the last cookie with a friend?

15

Sometimes friends want to play different things. When that happens, they take turns.

First Max and James play computer games for Max. Then they play soccer for James.

That's how they stay friends.

Sometimes friends may feel **angry**. When that happens, they can talk about how they feel.

Later, they can say, "I'm sorry."

That's what friends do!

Let's be friends!

angry

LET'S PLAY TOGETHER!

American Sign Language is a way of "talking" using signs made with your hands.

Come   play

ou can use American Sign Language to ask
friend to play. Here's how:

with

me!

YOUR NEW WORDS

angry (**ang**-gree) feeling like you
    want to fight with someone

friends (frends) people who like being
    together

laugh (laf) to make a sound that shows you
    think something is funny

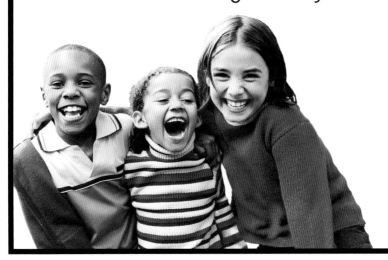

playground (**play**-ground) an outdoor area with swings, slides, or other places for children to play

puzzle (**puhz**-uhl) a game where you fit small pieces together to make one big picture

share (shair) to divide something between two or more people

smile (smile) to turn your mouth up at the corners to show you are happy

INDEX

FIND OUT MORE

Book:
Raschka, Chris. *Yo! Yes?* New York: Scholastic, 2007.

Website:
www.tolerance.org/pt/new_friend/index_friend.html

MEET THE AUTHOR
Amanda Miller is a writer and editor for Scholastic. She and her dog, Henry, live in Brooklyn, New York.